"This devotional will undoubtedly feed and fortify your soul. Tiffany's words reveal the magnificent substance of her soul, a beautiful blend of selfless humility, inner tenacity, and unwavering consistency. As a result of nourishing her soul, she is able to help others view every day experiences as opportunities for transformation. If you desire optimal soul health, this is a spiritual staple…Enjoy!"

-   *Colleen Swindoll-Thompson,* Director of Reframing Ministries (A Division of Insight for Living)

"There are days when what I need most is a quick word of encouragement from a trusted friend, someone who gets my reality and has a little wisdom and sanity to offer in the middle of my crazy schedule. The Go-Getter Devotional is just such a resource, and Tiffany Jo Baker the needed voice to pen it. Not only does she understand my day-to-day responsibilities, she also knows how to care for my soul. If you need a long drink of water, this devotional will provide it."

-   Michele Cushatt, author of Relentless: The Unshakeable Presence of a God Who Never Leaves

"Tiffany's devotional will inspire you to live beyond yourself and embrace the wild journey along the way. These daily encouragements will stir your faith and propel you forward in all that God has called you to do!"

-   *Sarah Birkbeck,* Founder of Refresh

31 DAY DEVOTIONAL

SOUL-CARE
for
GO-GETTERS

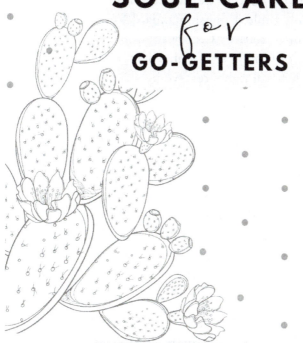

REFRESH AND REFOCUS
IN 5 MINUTES A DAY

TIFFANY JO BAKER

Dedication

I dedicate this devotional to my family, my biggest cheerleaders on my faith and go-getting journey. Dad and mom, thank you for always believing in me and teaching me to get God first. Brian, thank you for always saying yes to my ideas (most of them anyways) and picking up the slack while I am in the thick of going for it. Trinity and Selah, thank you for cheering me on and sharing your mommy time. I couldn't do any of this without you all and love you deeply.

Table of Contents

Introduction

When was the last time you felt refreshed or focused despite your ever-growing ideas and to-do list?

Sometimes I dream of these moments. Usually it involves me on a tropical beach or hiking up a mountain.

Then I wake up.

Maybe you can relate.

Your ideas are many and your life is full. You have purpose, plans and projects, but there is so much to do and so little time.

You know the dream is real, but so is the struggle.

Friend, it's time for a *powerful pause* and it can happen from the oh-so exotic location of your bed, office or kitchen.

In this 31-day devotional, relatable stories and bite-sized nuggets of wisdom will help you refresh in God's presence and refocus on His proven and tested ways of doing things.

Find peace and purpose in the morning moments with God to jump-start your day and get the right perspective before you tackle your to-dos.

Day 1:

The Middle Is Always Messy

I took pictures at the beginning, middle and end of the cabinet painting project party.

Counters full, cabinet insides exposed and exploding with stuff, I was almost embarrassed to share the pictures midway through the project.

The middle of a DIY project, spring cleaning, college degree, putting up your Christmas tree, or taking a leap of faith is always messy, but you aren't supposed to stop there. Too many people do.

It's so easy to get tired, weary and doubtful. Our body screams as if in the middle of a marathon, our mind yells looking logically at all that is happening around us and our heart cries out with insecurities.

That is the moment you have to *faith-it*. Put the end vision in front of you and focus on that. If you know deep down this is what you are supposed to do, don't give yourself the option to give in and give up.

Keep going, friend. You've got this.

"And I am sure of this, that he who began a good work in you will bring it to completion at the day of Jesus Christ" *(Philippians 1:6).*

· · · · · · ❖ · · · · · ·

Takeaway

What is God saying to you today?

• • • • • • ❖ • • • • • •

Declaration (go ahead, declare it and say it *out loud*)

God, thank You for being with me from the beginning to the end. I am confident in the call and fully walk it out courageously…

Day 2:

Transformed

One of my guilty pleasures is binge-watching home renovation, design and cooking shows on the weekends. I'm always amazed at how they take outdated, worn out, overlooked and simple everyday items and transform them into the opposite.

That's exactly what God does with us.

The control freak finds peace.
The perfectionist finds mercy.
The abused finds gentleness.
The insecure finds confidence.
The shy finds their voice.
The unsure finds direction.
The trapped finds freedom.
The overwhelmed finds clarity.
The weary finds rest.

You will find what you are missing, friend. He will take those broken, hard places and make them like new.

"You have turned for me my mourning into dancing; you have loosed my sackcloth and clothed me with gladness." (Psalm 30:11).

Takeaway

What is God saying to you today?

• • • • • • • ❖ • • • • • • •

Declaration (go ahead, declare it and say it *out loud*)

God, thank You for Your life-giving work in me. I am transformed…

Day 3:

Life Is an Adventure

While flying in a little Alaska float plane last summer, the pilot had us wear headphones.

As we traveled over water and glaciers to a lodge only accessible by sea plane, the headphones served two big purposes. They blocked out the loud engine noise and allowed us to hear a pre-recorded message from the pilot about what we were seeing and about to experience on our journey.

Friend, today I want you to grab your headphones and get ready!

Get in your quiet place and allow God, The Pilot, to block out all the unnecessary life noise and speak to you about your journey—where you are at and where you are going.

There are some sweet destinations in life that can only be accessed from these times, not to mention the turbulence that can be avoided.

My prayer for you is that you connect with your Creator and soar this week, friend.

"The heart of man plans his way, but the LORD establishes his steps" (Proverbs 16:9).

Takeaway

What is God saying to you today?

• • • • • • • ❖ • • • • • • •

Declaration (go ahead, declare it and say it *out loud*)

God, thank You for speaking to me and directing my steps. My steps are ordered and secure…

Day 4:

Hit the Repeat Button

It took a minute. Ok, more than that for the initial shock of the doctor's diagnosis of epilepsy for our youngest daughter to fade to where I could breathe again, swallow again and reason again.

What's the right thing to do in those circumstances, when you are unexpectedly hit with awful news? When the problem is visible, but the purpose is still hidden? When all you can see is the devastation and you don't know why this is happening or what to do yet?

The best thing you can do is to dig deep. Pull out those old memories of His faithfulness and hold on for dear life to the goodness of His heart. Friend, remind yourself of His truth...

He is good (Exodus 34:6).
His mercy never ends (Psalm 136:1).
His love always works (1 Corinthians 13:8).
He knows the end from the beginning (Isaiah 46:10).
He is always with you (Hebrews 13:5).

Then, slowly but surely it becomes as simple as, "I trust You, Jesus."

Now put this phrase on repeat in your mind, your heart and your lips.

Takeaway

What is God saying to you today?

● ● ● ● ● ● ● ❖ ● ● ● ● ● ● ●

Declaration (go ahead, declare it and say it *out loud*)

God, thank You for Your faithfulness. You have proven Yourself over and over to me. I trust You, Jesus…

Day 5:

Fix Your Eyes Forward

Trinity was only in preschool, but she had wisdom beyond her years.

We were driving in our minivan when this small, yet confidant voice shared from the back to all who would listen...

"Mom, if you look out the side window it looks like we are going really fast, but if you look out the front window, it looks like we are going really slow."

Boy, was she right. Sometimes, when we are focused on the right things (where we are going with our eyes fixed on Jesus), it can seem like our progress is going soooo slow. In reality, we are moving forward and flying past a lot of stuff that could distract, demolish and even detour us along the way.

> *Therefore, since we are surrounded by such a great cloud of witnesses, let us throw off every encumbrance and the sin that so easily entangles, and let us run with endurance the race set out for us.* **Let us fix our eyes on Jesus**, *the author and perfecter of our faith, who* **for the joy set before Him** *endured the cross, scorning its shame, and sat down at the right hand of the throne of God. Consider Him who endured such hostility from sinners, so that you will not grow weary and lose heart (Hebrews 12:1-3, Berean Study Bible, emphasis mine).*

• • • • • • • ❖ • • • • • • •

If Jesus, during the hardest parts of His ministry on earth, had to keep His focus on the good things to come so He would fulfill what He was called to do, so do you and I!

Takeaway

What is God saying to you today?

● ● ● ● ● ● ● ❖ ● ● ● ● ● ● ●

Declaration (go ahead, declare it and say it *out loud*)

God, my eyes are fixed on You. I don't look back, I keep my focus forward while doing what You have called me to do and I trust You with the timing…

Day 6:

Get Back Up

I didn't know if I could handle one more thing.

We were in a tough season, in the middle of a leap of faith and all hell seemed to be breaking loose. So, I started keeping a list on my phone. Not to keep track of all that was going wrong, but to keep a list of all the things God would redeem and Satan would have to repay.

When we are daily fighting the good fight and doing the things God has put on our heart to do, from the home to the office, it can be hard and downright suck.

I want to remind you...

You are righteous.
You are brave.
You are bold.

"For the righteous falls seven times and rises again, but the wicked stumble in times of calamity" (Proverbs 24:16).

"The wicked flee when no one pursues, but the righteous are bold as a lion" (Proverbs 28:1).

Keep getting up, my fierce friend. You are not alone.

• • • • • • • ❖ • • • • • • •

Takeaway

What is God saying to you today?

• • • • • • • ❖ • • • • • • •

Declaration (go ahead, declare it and say it *out loud*)

God, thank You for empowering me to do what You called me to do. I am righteous, brave and bold and get back up every time…

Day 7:

Peace Is Priceless

Every Thanksgiving we go around the table saying one thing we are thankful for. Year after year my answer has been the same. Peace.

Peace is a unique thing though...

You know when you have it and you know when it's missing. It creates a mood, a feeling, a stance and an atmosphere.

You never really know how valuable peace is until you've lived a period of time without it.

Yet, you can have it even in the middle of a storm.

Jesus is the Prince of Peace. He grew up on this earth and lived a regular life. When He ascended to heaven, He could've left us anything. Yet, knowing what life on earth was like, He chose to leave us His gift of peace.

"Peace I leave with you; my peace I give to you" (John 14:27a).

Open the free gift, friend. It's priceless.

Takeaway

What is God saying to you today?

• • • • • • • ❖ • • • • • • •

Declaration (go ahead, declare it and say it *out loud*)

God, thank You for Your Peace. I choose to accept and utilize the gift You have given me. I am peace-full…

Day 8:

Unmovable

I did a piece of scary and put myself out there.

That's a vulnerable thing for a writer and speaker. It reminded me of the first day of junior high, walking into the cafeteria.

I wish I could say the response was outstanding. Sadly, it wasn't.

Mostly nothing, the sound of crickets, mixed only with criticism from one of my biggest cheerleaders.

I took a minute to feel the disappointment and then I remembered Who I was doing all this for.

Despite the feelings...
-the unknowns
-the fears
-the failures
-the disabilities
-the past
-the concerns

The fact remains, the Lord Almighty is with us and we are created and called by Him.

Though the storm rages, your bills keep coming, the heat is turned up, your insecurities are on display....

You will not fall. You will not fear. You will not give up.

He is your fortress and you will not be moved.

"God is within her, she will not fall" (Psalm 46:5, NIV).

Takeaway

What is God saying to you today?

• • • • • • • ❖ • • • • • • •

Declaration (go ahead, declare it and say it *out loud*)

God, thank You for always being with me. I am unmoved by what is happening around me and stand confidently in Your presence and purpose…

Day 9:

New to You, But Not New to Him

It was my first day on the job. New place, new boss, new team and new role.

New situations and seasons can bring up old insecurities, even hidden under a new outfit.

Although an opportunity or experience may be new to you, it's not new to God.

New is His specialty.

"Behold, I am doing a new thing; now it springs forth, do you not perceive it? I will make a way in the wilderness and rivers in the desert" (Isaiah 43:19).

He makes all things new.

"And He who was seated on the throne said, 'Behold, I am making all things new.' Also he said, 'Write this down, for these words are trustworthy and true'" (Revelation 21:5).

His mercies are new every morning.

"The steadfast love of the LORD never ceases; his mercies never come to an end; they are new every morning; great is your faithfulness" (Lamentations 3:22–23).

He doesn't change.

"Jesus Christ is the same yesterday and today and forever" (Hebrews 13:8).

•••••• ❖ ••••••

You can trust Him and stand confident knowing that God is with you. He has created and equipped you and He knows the end from the beginning.

Soul-Care for Go-Getters

Takeaway

What is God saying to you today?

• • • • • • • ❖ • • • • • • •

Declaration (go ahead, declare it and say it *out loud*)

God, thank You that You go before, beside and behind me, guiding and guarding the way. I am secure, confident and experience Your mercies afresh and anew today and every day…

Day 10:

Your Part Is the Obedience, God's Part Is the Outcome

I had thrown my all into it.

Lots of money, time and energy.

I quit my job in faith to pursue what God had put on my heart to do. Everyone else made the online entrepreneurial world look so easy and gave me a simple formula that was supposed to work for me too.

But it didn't.

Crickets chirping. That's pretty much all I got out of it.

I was disappointed, hurt and now questioning everything.

Ever been there too?

As go-getters, we strive for the results we want. Seems easy, right? A+B should equal C. We've been taught that since kindergarten.

But, in the real world, a formulaic approach doesn't always work and the results aren't up to us. There is a part we can do and there is a part we can't do.

Your part is the obedience to do what God and His

• • • • • • • ❖ • • • • • • •

wisdom has led you to do and the rest is up to God. He knows the end from the beginning. He has an elevated eternal perspective and knows how each of the pieces fit together from the beginning to the end. His timing is perfect.

"Commit your way to the LORD; trust in him, and he will act." (Psalm 37:5).

Trust God with today's results and tomorrow's destinations.

Easier said than done, I know. But there is freedom, peace and focus in knowing whose responsibility is whose.

Friend, stay in your lane. God's got this.

Takeaway

What is God saying to you today?

• • • • • • • ❖ • • • • • • •

Declaration (go ahead, declare it and say it *out loud*)

God, thank You for leading me to know what I'm supposed to do in this season. I am being obedient to do it and I trust that You will be faithful with the right results today and tomorrow...

Day 11:

You Are Not Forgotten

It was my birthday.

In the past year I had graduated from college, gotten married and moved halfway across the country to start a new life and job.

Besides my husband, no one remembered my birthday where we were living until the morning after. A local friend called apologetically. She told me God had given her a dream the night before about it being my birthday.

My heart was touched that during a lonely and difficult season God would remind someone about me.

The word "remember" is used 231 times in the Bible (NIV). Over and over the Bible tells us that "God remembered" His people and promises and that we should remember His faithfulness and covenant.

When the Bible says that God "remembers" something or someone, it doesn't mean He had forgotten them and just started thinking about them again. It means He turned His attention to someone and acted on their behalf.

Soul-Care for Go-Getters

God remembered Noah and sent a wind to dry up the water (Genesis 8:1).

God remembered Rachel and opened her womb (Genesis 30:22).

How cool is it that the God of the Universe thinks about you and acts on your behalf, even when you feel invisible or forgotten!

When He thinks about you, He thinks thoughts of peace and what He can do to give you hope for your future (Jeremiah 29:11).

He thinks about you so much that if you counted His thoughts about you, they would outnumber the grains of sand (Psalm 139: 17–18).

Friend, you are not forgotten. You have a Heavenly Father who thinks good thoughts about you constantly and acts on your behalf to make things happen for you according to His masterful and timely plan.

Takeaway

What is God saying to you today?

• • • • • • • ❖ • • • • • • •

Declaration (go ahead, declare it and say it *out loud*)

God, thank You for never forsaking or forgetting me.
I am not alone and have a bright future…

Day 12:

Divine Detour or Deterring Distraction

Have you ever wondered why house cleaners can clean so quickly?

A handful of times a year, when life is extra full, I treat myself and family to getting our house professionally cleaned.

Every time, I am stunned at how quickly they get it done. It takes me twice as long. It takes my kids two to four times as long.

Then I realized ... I get distracted by all the things; my internal to-do list, a text, laundry, paperwork pile, hungry dog, a chocolate chip cookie calling me from the kitchen. The list goes on. And don't get me started on all the things that distract our children.

But not the cleaners. They come in *focused, with a plan and purpose.*

This is how a lot of us become less effective than we could be. We let life and stuff (even good stuff) distract us from what we are supposed to be doing.

To add to it, the enemy may throw in distractions too—unforgiveness, comparison, hurts, jealousy, doubt, lack and insecurities.

• • • • • • • ❖ • • • • • • •

You have to choose to stay in mama-bear protection mode of your goals and purpose and quickly determine when things pop up if they are divine detours or deterring distractions so you won't get off track and ineffective.

"My sheep hear my voice, and I know them, and they follow me" (John 10:27).

You have a divine purpose, friend. Stay focused.

Takeaway

What is God saying to you today?

• • • • • • • ❖ • • • • • • •

Declaration (go ahead, declare it and say it *out loud*)

God, thank You that I know Your voice and You lead me so that I can't be deterred or distracted from the purpose and plan You have for my life...

Day 13:

Better Together

None of us were created with all we need, to do all we were created to do.

I think that is one of the biggest lessons I learned from the amazingly strong women whose babies I carried as a gestational carrier (aka surrogate).

It takes a village to raise kids, build businesses and birth dreams.

We were each created with a specific set of giftings and purpose. Then mix in your unique personality and different experiences and you become a one-of-a-kind dream maker team player.

"For as in one body we have many members, and the members do not all have the same function, so we, though many, are one body in Christ, and individually members one of another. Having gifts that differ according to the grace given to us, let us use them" (Romans 12:4-6a).

If you are doing life, ministry or business alone, there is a better way. You need me and I need you.

We are better together.

• • • • • • • ❖ • • • • • • •

Takeaway

What is God saying to you today?

• • • • • • • ❖ • • • • • • •

Declaration (go ahead, declare it and say it *out loud*)

God, thank You for making me with a divine plan and purpose in mind. I am created, called and equipped to join with others to make a difference…

Day 14:

Learn to Rest, Not Quit

I couldn't do one more thing. I was at the point where the song, "All I Want To Be is Done" by The Band Perry was becoming my battle cry. I was:

Overwhelmed.
Busy.
Stressed.
Weary.
Worn-out.
Exhausted.
Depleted.
Done.

Have you been there too? Or maybe you are there right now.

We fight for positions, relationships, significance, finances, dreams, survival and even others, but do we fight for boundaries, balance and health (spirit, soul and body) for ourselves and loved ones?

Resting is a skill. Something to be learned, valued and implemented.

Instead of always filling your schedule with something, today fill it with strategic periods of "nothing." Rest will keep you at your best.

Soul-Care for Go-Getters

"Come to me, all who labor and are heavy laden, and I will give you rest" (Matthew 11:28).

Takeaway

What is God saying to you today?

• • • • • • • ❖ • • • • • • •

Declaration (go ahead, declare it and say it *out loud*)

God, You designed seasons and cycles. Help me to value and fight for times of rest. I am at my best when I am refreshed and following Your plan for my life…

Day 15:

The Simple Isn't Always Easy

I've been feeling a little off.

I was thinking it might be my hormones (yay birth control), interrupted sleep or maybe my growing to-do list.

Maybe it was the aftermath of removing over 200 ticks from our dog after our time at the cabin last weekend or the fact that we just found out we are moving.

Honestly, I was hoping it was one of those "easy fixes," but I knew that wasn't it.

When it came down to it, I wasn't spending time reading God's Word like I normally do. I justified it with listening to constant praise music and preachers on YouTube, but that didn't fill me all the way.

Do you have those seasons too? When you are feeding your spirit in some ways, but you know you need more?

Some seasons take more to fill up than others. My cup, and yours, can only overflow from time in His presence and His Word. It's a simple, yet difficult solution in a very noisy world. But it is so worth it.

• • • • • • • ❖ • • • • • • •

"You make known to me the path of life; in your presence there is fullness of joy; at your right hand are pleasures forevermore" (Psalm 16:11).

• • • • • • • ❖ • • • • • • •

Takeaway

What is God saying to you today?

(blank lined writing space)

• • • • • • • ❖ • • • • • • •

Declaration (go ahead, declare it and say it *out loud*)

God, thank You for Your life-giving and illuminating Word. Nothing fills me like You do. I am filled to overflowing in Your presence…

Day 16:

The Power of a Pivot

Remember the famous *Friends* TV show scene with Ross yelling "pivot" as the roommates try to move his new sofa up the 90-degree staircase?

Although Ross seemed to make this word and concept famous almost overnight, it has been around since biblical times. In fact, there is a Psalm in the Bible known as The Pivot Psalm!

The definition of pivot is "the central point, pin or shaft on which a mechanism turns or oscillates[1]."

In an attempt to keep the Word of God sacred and with integrity, the Jews would count every chapter and verse to make sure nothing was added or taken away from the original Scriptures.

The exact middle of the Old Testament is said to be the first verse of Psalm 103. That is how this verse came to be known as The Pivot Psalm.

It is the central point of the Old Testament, the center of our Christianity. I don't believe it is an accident that the focus of this central pivot verse, the one we can hang our faith and hope on is all about praise; praising our God and His amazing love and character towards us.

● ● ● ● ● ● ● ✧ ● ● ● ● ● ● ●

"Bless the LORD, O my soul, and all that is within me, bless his holy name!" (Psalm 103:1, aka The Pivot Psalm).

Next time you hear the word pivot, let it result in a praise.

[1]Oxford University Press, "Pivot: Definition of Pivot by Oxford Dictionary on Lexico.com Also Meaning of Pivot," Lexico Dictionaries | English (Lexico Dictionaries, 2020), https://www.lexico.com/en/definition/pivot.

• • • • • • • ❖ • • • • • • •

Takeaway

What is God saying to you today?

• • • • • • • ❖ • • • • • • •

Declaration (go ahead, declare it and say it *out loud*)

God, thank You for who You are, all You have done and for the many blessings You have given me. You are a good God. I am truly blessed and thankful to You...

Day 17:

Firm Footing (Even in Wedges, Heels and Flip-Flops)

I'm the kind of girl that has the gift of tripping over nothing. Needless to say, I rarely wear heels. Our girls, since they were toddlers, would come out of my closet with my dress shoes on, walking more confidently and gracefully than I ever have, even though you could fit three of their feet into one of my shoes. Other than that, my heels mostly collect dust in my closet.

I remember walking down the aisle on my wedding day in heels. One of the main thoughts running through my head was, "Don't trip, don't trip, don't trip." Even though I was uncomfortable and unstable in my heels, I took strength, comfort and confidence while walking down the aisle because I was holding onto my father's arm the entire time.

> *For who is God, but the LORD?*
> *And who is a rock, except our God,*
> *The God who girds me with strength*
> *And makes my way blameless?*
> **He makes my feet like hinds' feet,**
> *And sets me upon my high places [...]*
> *You enlarge my steps under me,*
> *And my feet have not slipped*
> *(Psalm 18: 31-33, 36, NASB).*

Soul-Care for Go-Getters

A hind is a red female deer. They are the most sure-footed mountain animal, effortlessly able to move through the mountains without stumbling.

God equips us with sure footing, despite the difficult terrain we may be treading or the shoes we may be wearing. Your feet will not slip, no matter the path you are on because you have a steady, firm foundation in your Heavenly Father's grip.

Keep going, friend. God is with you and holding you up each step of the way.

• • • • • • • ❖ • • • • • • •

Takeaway

What is God saying to you today?

• • • • • • • ❖ • • • • • • •

Declaration (go ahead, declare it and say it *out loud*)

God, thank You for directing and strengthening my steps. I am never alone…

Day 18:

Satan Is After Your Smile

It was the fourth grade, the first time I remember being ashamed and embarrassed to smile, yet I didn't fully understand why.

One of the popular boys called me a name—a name I didn't understand, but I understood the context and the snickers from his guy friends. A name that called out my full lips. A name that kept me from smiling that year for school pictures—instead, I held my lips in to make them look smaller.

That was the first time I can remember Satan trying to steal my smile.

Since then there have been many moments I have been utterly crushed, my smile, my joy hidden by the wounds of a diagnosis, relationship issues and real life woes.

I'm convinced; Satan is after our smile.

You see, you can have some faith without joy. We've seen those Christians in the fight and we have been there before too.

But you can't have a lot of faith without joy.

I learned years ago, during an especially trying time, that my joy was connected to my faith. Joy and faith are a dynamic duo, two powerful forces that

synergistically work together. To have one without the other is like having dynamite without a fuse. A gun without the bullets.

Joy is the cup of coffee to your daily to-do list. It will keep you going. It will keep you from giving up. It will keep you strong in the fight. It will be contagious and draw others into the Kingdom. It will make the fight and the journey do-able, memorable and, dare I say it, enjoyable.

You may be in the battle today. You may be fighting the good fight. You may be believing and standing in faith. If so, the most powerful thing you can do for your faith is support it with joy!

Protect your joy at all costs. Friend, don't let Satan steal your smile.

"The joy of the Lord is your strength" (Nehemiah 8:10b).

Takeaway

What is God saying to you today?

• • • • • • • ❖ • • • • • • •

Declaration (go ahead, declare it and say it *out loud*)

God, thank You for Your joy and the strength it provides to my faith and daily life. I am joy-full...

Day 19:

You Can Do Anything, but Not Everything

Driving home from the birthday party, I thought about the table of ladies that had just celebrated and spoken life into the newest adult at the table. As I remembered the things I shared with this eighteen year old, a quote came to my mind and summed it all up perfectly…

You can do anything, but you can't (and shouldn't) do everything.

Whew!

I don't know about you, but this quote relieves me, excites me and empowers me.

Friend, YOU CAN DO ANYTHING.

You were created to soar; the sky is the limit. Go after the things God has put in your heart and don't quit until you know God is opening a different door.

Friend, YOU CAN'T DO EVERYTHING.

In order to do the things you were divinely created to do, you have to know your season, your purpose and what matters most to you.

There are only 24 hours in a day; no matter what, that won't change. But you get to choose what you do in those minutes to make them count.

"For everything there is a season, and a time for every matter under heaven" (Ecclesiastes 3:1).

Takeaway

What is God saying to you today?

• • • • • • • ❖ • • • • • • •

Declaration (go ahead, declare it and say it *out loud*)

God, thank You for the abilities and opportunities You have given me. I am directed and empowered to do the things You have created me to do…

Day 20:

The Math of Marriage

Let's just say I wasn't the easiest catch.

There was a lot I went through, overcame and healed from before I was at a place where I was whole enough by myself, with just me and God.

The biblical meaning of "two becoming one" has been misrepresented and misunderstood.

It doesn't mean that you become whole when you find your man.
It doesn't mean that two half people become one whole person.
It doesn't mean that you were incomplete on your own.

It means that you now choose to join together, to be aligned, unified, to reproduce exponentially, be merged into a powerful unit that thinks and acts together ... no longer just for yourself.

It isn't 1+1=1

or even 1/2 +1/2=1

It's multiplication! It's an exponential increase that begins with 1x1=1.

• • • • • • • ❖ • • • • • • •

And when you add the Lord in the center and both of you have hearts to do marriage, love and life His way, get ready for an adventure.

> *Two are better than one, because they have a good return for their labor: if either of them falls down, one can help the other up. But pity anyone who falls and has no one to help them up. Also, if two lie down together, they will keep warm. But how can one keep warm alone? Though one may be overpowered, two can defend themselves. A cord of three strands is not quickly broken (Ecclesiastes 4:9–12, NIV).*

You + Your Spouse + God = A Dream Team

Takeaway

What is God saying to you today?

• • • • • • ❖ • • • • • •

Declaration (go ahead, declare it and say it *out loud*)

God, thank You for the power of multiplication when I join my life and vision with You and my husband. You make me whole and I am unified with my husband for great Kingdom purpose…

Day 21:

Recharged and Ready

I couldn't figure it out.

Something was draining my cell phone battery at warp speed. It was only mid-day and I was already getting the flashing red battery level warnings.

I didn't have a charger and my phone just died.

I'm sure you can relate. Where were you the last time you were left with a dead phone? In a smartphone, tech-based connected world, our phones have to stay charged!

Friend, it's the same with us.

We only have a limited battery life before needing to recharge.

Some things will drain us faster than others.
Some things will charge us back up faster than others.

Are you recharging your battery to 100% daily or are you starting on empty?

You can't give from a dead battery. You have to stay full so that you have something to give and are able to do what you were created to do.

"He refreshes my soul" (Psalm 23:3a, NIV).

Takeaway

What is God saying to you today?

● ● ● ● ● ● ● ❖ ● ● ● ● ● ● ●

Declaration (go ahead, declare it and say it *out loud*)

God, I know I can't do this life without You. Help me to recharge moment by moment and day by day. I am refreshed and refocused in Your presence…

Day 22:

Be All In

Where are my frugal friends at?

I head straight to the clearance rack, use coupons and promo codes when possible and conserve all the good-expensive stuff I have.

Like skin care.

When it says to use two pumps of facial serum, I moderately use one, trying to get two months out of the expensive product.

Although my skin is better and I'm seeing a difference, I'm not experiencing the full results the manufacturer designed and instructed.

I wonder if there are other parts of my life where I am giving and getting only half the results I could be?

What about you?

We have our Creator's instruction book for full and abundant functioning. When we decide to do things our way or not be all in to His, we don't experience the optimal results and then may wonder why.

"The thief comes only to steal and kill and destroy; I have come that they may have life, and have it to the full" (John 10:10, NIV).

Don't cheat yourself or your results. Be all in.

Takeaway
What is God saying to you today?

• • • • • • ❖ • • • • • •

Declaration (go ahead, declare it and say it *out loud*)

God, today I choose to be all in to Your will and Your way. Thank You for the full life that is found in You…

Day 23:

Find Your Sweet Spot

I have this thing.

It's not something I talk about a lot, but it's something that is always in the back of my mind.

We all have those things. Some would call them lemons. It may not be a defective car, but it may be something that just popped up, always with you or a behind the scenes pest that hits when you are weakest or least expect it.

So what do we do when life gives us lemons?

We squeeze them.

It's time to put pressure on your lemons and start getting something good out of them. It's a way to reframe your lemons and your life.

Instead of letting your lemons steal your joy, energy, relationships and whatever else, it's time for you to tell the voice about your lemons to be quiet and that you are no longer letting them steal the sweetness from your life. It's time for you to see the sweet things that this sour spot can bring.

Maybe this lemon has brought a new friendship, a new level of faith, a new vulnerability, a new strength, a new hope, a new perspective. Take a minute now to think about the good stuff that this lemon has or could bring to your life (if you let it).

Lemons are a crucial ingredient to making lemonade, but you have to add the sugar to the lemons. That's your part. Find your sugar. Find your sweet spot.

God didn't cause the lemons, but He can help you add the sugar.

"Set your minds on things that are above, not on things that are on earth" (Colossians 3:2).

Takeaway

What is God saying to you today?

Declaration (go ahead, declare it and say it *out loud*)

God, thank You for helping me see the good that You are bringing from this tough place. I choose to focus my thoughts, energy and words on what is good and when I can't find the good, I trust You with the process...

Day 24:

Pay Now or Pay Later

I forgot what it was like.

We got a new puppy who needs to learn how to go potty outside, sleep in her puppy condo (aka crate) and play nice with her fur-sister.

When she rings the bell on the back door, I know most of the time she doesn't have to go to the bathroom; she just wants to chase the birds and bunnies.

It would be so much easier to just ignore the bell ring. That would allow me to get more work done today, but in the long run, what would that be teaching her?

Even though our bad habits develop from understandable (and sometimes needed) quick wins and give-ins, it's easy to forget that most often bad habits are harder to break than daily discipline is to develop from the start.

Said differently, "Choose your ruts wisely; you'll be in them a long time"[2] or You will either pay the price now or pay the price later.

This is applicable for everything from your bedtime routines for kiddos, priorities, time together as spouses, finances and goal-getting, to food and fitness, potty training and following through on discipline. The list could go on and on.

It's so easy to give in because, let's face it, you are exhausted as parents, leaders and humans.

At the end of the day consistency and being a person of your word *is* important, but don't forget to mix it with a big dose of grace, mercy and choosing your battles wisely.

"Therefore, my beloved brothers, be steadfast, immovable, always abounding in the work of the Lord, knowing that in the Lord your labor is not in vain" (1 Corinthians 15:58).

---

[2] Les Parrott, *Saving Your Marriage before It Starts* (Grand Rapids, MI: Zondervan, 2015).

Takeaway

What is God saying to you today?

• • • • • • • ❖ • • • • • • •

Declaration (go ahead, declare it and say it *out loud*)

God, thank You for the tenacity and self-control I need to do what You've called me to do. I am faithful with the little things and it will make a big difference for Your glory…

Day 25:

In Good Times and Bad

I got the call.

My numbers had dropped. One day I was pregnant, the next I wasn't.

As a three-time surrogate, I was supposed to be the proven professional. I was supposed to be the answer to many prayers, sleepless nights and family dreams. Instead, I was crushed. My heart hurt for the intended parents as I laid in a pile of tears on my bed.

Loss had left me feeling all alone.

But I knew I wasn't. God was with me and He understood.

He gets it when you are in severe pain.

He gets it when you lose a loved one.
He gets it when people betray you.
He gets it when people misunderstand you.
He gets it when you aren't promoted.
He gets it when your heart longs for different.
He gets it when you need a miracle.

Jesus understands suffering. He doesn't cause it, but He gets it.

"He was despised and rejected by men, a man of sorrows and acquainted with grief; and as one from whom men hide their faces he was despised, and we esteemed him not" (Isaiah 53:3).

Not only does He understand, but He is with you in those moments. Yes, our God is the God of the miraculous and impossible, but He is also the God who is with us in our pain and suffering. He's the God of the hills and valleys.

He is with you each step of the way. Immanuel, God with us (Matthew 1:23).

Takeaway

What is God saying to you today?

• • • • • • • ❖ • • • • • • •

Declaration (go ahead, declare it and say it *out loud*)

God, thank You for being a God who understands what I am going through and standing with me through the ups and downs. I am understood and never alone...

Day 26:

Don't Trust Your Progress, Trust His Promise

It was my 40th birthday.

My hubby started celebrating me by sharing some nice things at dinner with my family. I started crying. Not happy tears. Although the things he was saying were great and true, I was not happy with where I was in life. I thought I would be further along by now.

It's easy to get discouraged when we look at the gap between where we are and where we want to be. It can look like a deep chasm, almost uncrossable.

It's especially hard for dream makers and goal getters because we are constantly giving our all towards the goal. We are focused on the numbers, the results and the bottom line.

But God …

God isn't dissuaded by the natural or the process. Time doesn't hold Him back. He is famous for being a God who "suddenly" makes a way. These "suddenlies" often happened after a time of faithfulness and seeking the Lord, prayer and trusting God.

Friend, rest not in your ability, but in His promise and purpose for you. And keep being faithful as you wait.

Soul-Care for Go-Getters

• • • • • • • ❖ • • • • • • •

"About midnight Paul and Silas were praying and singing hymns to God, and the prisoners were listening to them, and suddenly there was a great earthquake, so that the foundations of the prison were shaken. And immediately all the doors were opened, and everyone's bonds were unfastened" (Acts 16:25-26).

Takeaway

What is God saying to you today?

• • • • • • • ❖ • • • • • • •

Declaration (go ahead, declare it and say it *out loud*)

God, I trust Your timing, Your will and Your ways. I choose to be faithful through the process and seek You each step of the way until You "suddenly" break through on my behalf…

Day 27:

Hot-Mess Express

Nine school zones in 7.8 miles.

That's the morning commute to my office.

Can you imagine? I'm sure you can. You have some too. Maybe not school zones, but those things that slow you down when you are on a purposeful mission.

We could let these things frustrate us, or we could choose to see them differently.

Now, every time I hit the breaks for a school zone, I pray. Just a simple shout-out to the Lord for protection, wisdom and direction for those in the school. Even during the holidays when school is out of session and the lights are still unnecessarily flashing.

This practice helps to tame my hot mess, one school zone at a time.

How can you reframe and repurpose the frustrating situations that seem to be delaying your mission?

"And we know that for those who love God all things work together for good, for those who are called according to his purpose" (Romans 8:28).

• • • • • • • ❖ • • • • • • •

Takeaway

What is God saying to you today?

• • • • • • • ❖ • • • • • • •

Declaration (go ahead, declare it and say it *out loud*)

God, thank You for Your love and patience towards me. I choose today to see the good and be used to bring good from even the frustrating situations around me...

Day 28:

Designed for Optimal Performance

I started getting the warning message on my phone again: "It's been seven days since you last restarted your phone. We recommended you shut off and restart your phone."

Had it really been that long since I restarted my phone? Time passes so quickly that I often forget. Although I never see the warning on my phone at an opportune time to restart it, I always appreciate the reminder.

God instituted a similar manufacturer recommendation in His manual for us and He called it the sabbath.

"And on the seventh day God finished his work that He had done, and he rested on the seventh day from all His work that he had done" (Genesis 2:2).

You are like a cell phone.

What are you doing to protect and reset your performance every seven days in order to carry out the Manufacturer's recommendations for optimal function and longevity?

Takeaway

What is God saying to you today?

● ● ● ● ● ● ● ❖ ● ● ● ● ● ● ●

Declaration (go ahead, declare it and say it *out loud*)

God, thank You for always looking out for my spirit, soul and body. Help me to rest and reset. When I do things Your way, I am unstoppable...

Day 29:

Pressure Makes Diamonds

Sometimes I can feel it.

The weight of the season. The magnitude of the decisions, position and responsibilities.

Sometimes I want to run, or better yet, dig a hole and hide in it.

But I just can't. I have been around long enough to know that hidden in the dark parts of life are gems.

Like diamonds that form in the depths of the earth from high heat and extreme pressure, sometimes these seasons are preparing us to shine.

Friend, if you are in a deep dark place, feeling a tremendous weight and the heat has been turned up, you may be in the right position for something beautiful to form.

"Out of the depths I cry to you, O LORD! O Lord, hear my voice! Let your ears be attentive to the voice of my pleas for mercy!" (Psalm 130:1-2).

Takeaway

What is God saying to you today?

• • • • • • • ✤ • • • • • • •

Declaration (go ahead, declare it and say it *out loud*)

God, thank You for Your faithfulness. You are with me in the good times and bad, on the mountain and in the valley. I take comfort in Your good plans and purpose for me...

Day 30:

Full, Fierce and Disciplined

It hit me. My mama-bear mode quickly and quietly turned on. Our baby girl was being targeted. It was at a varsity volleyball tournament game. The opposing side coach slyly pointed to a spot on our court for her server to target.

It was right where Trinity was, a large open area, where she stood all by herself.

I have been to many games and watched many coaches signal to their servers, but today was different.

I saw the opponent.
I saw their play.
I saw their motive.
I saw the opening.
I saw the weak spot.
I saw my daughter.

I wanted to say something.
I wanted to protect her.
I wanted to warn her.
I wanted to shield her.

But then it hit me. This is exactly what she has been trained for. She wasn't alone. There were five other teammates on the court who had her back, a coach

watching from a strategic vantage point calling the plays and other teammates sitting on the sidelines cheering her on.

My heart rested in the process as I watched, knowing that a tournament is made up of many plays, sets and matches and this was a moment they were ready for.

Friend, you may not be playing volleyball today, but the enemy of your soul may be hitting you right where it hurts. He will try to make a play against your weak spot. But you are not alone.

You have us, your brothers and sisters in Christ who have your back and are cheering you on. Most importantly, you have The Coach, watching from an eternal, heavenly perspective guiding you play by play.

You know what is coming.
Guard your heart.
Take your position.
Stay full, fierce and disciplined.

You are on the winning side.

"Be sober-minded; be watchful. Your adversary the devil prowls around like a roaring lion, seeking someone to devour. Resist him, firm in your faith" (1 Peter 5:8-9a).

•••••• ❖ ••••••

Takeaway

What is God saying to you today?

• • • • • • • ✥ • • • • • • •

Declaration (go ahead, declare it and say it *out loud*)

God, thank You for Your continued protection and direction and for people who love and support me. I am on the winning team…

Day 31:

Never Too Late

I'm not sure when my love for them started.

Somewhere in the last twenty years of living in Texas, the state plant, the Prickly Pear Cactus, has become my favorite.

It has turned me into a cacti and succulent lover.

But the love went to a "whole 'notha level" when I experienced and almost missed the true-to-form, 24-hour, big, bright yellow flower bloom on my cactus.

Every cactus has the ability to bloom, but it will only happen if they are mature and experiencing the proper conditions.

Some cacti don't bloom until they are 30, 40 or 50 years old. Those who aren't mature and under the right conditions will never bloom.

I'm in my forties, so this gives me hope (and it should to you too)! We have all been created with the capacity and ability to bloom; we just need to put ourselves in the right conditions to mature, grow and make it happen.

What are you doing today to invest in your maturity and growth in the areas that still need to bloom?

"And let us not grow weary of doing good, for in due season we will reap, if we do not give up" (Galatians 6:9).

Takeaway

What is God saying to you today?

• • • • • • ❖ • • • • • •

Declaration (go ahead, declare it and say it *out loud*)

God, thank You that Your timing is perfect and it's never too late. I will be faithful to do my part and trust You to do Yours...

Friend, you are loved and believed in!

I hope this doesn't stop our journey together. I would love to continue helping you fuel and fulfill your faith journey through the ups and downs.

Are you part of a group or team that believes in the power of investing in your soul and success? Maybe you are creatives, entrepreneurs, network marketing mamas, ministry leaders or a small group of women at church that would benefit from doing this devotional together.

If so, check out my **Go-Getter Group Study Pack** and other reminders and resources to help women like you with full hearts and full plates, refresh and refocus at www.TiffanyJoBaker.com/go-getters-devo.

Cheering you on,

Tiffany

P.S. I would LOVE to hear how God used this devotional and your takeaways! Send me a quick message on Instagram or Facebook at @TiffanyJoBaker.

Made in the USA
Middletown, DE
21 December 2020